YOU CHOOSE

GREAT ESCAPES

CAN YOU SURVIVE A CIVIL WAR ESCAPE?

AN INTERACTIVE HISTORY ADVENTURE

BY JESSICA GUNDERSON

CAPSTONE PRESS
a capstone imprint

Published by Capstone Press, an imprint of Capstone
1710 Roe Crest Drive, North Mankato, Minnesota 56003
capstonepub.com

Library of Congress Cataloging-in-Publication Data
Names: Gunderson, Jessica, author.
Title: Can you survive a Civil War escape? : an interactive history adventure / by Jessica Gunderson.
Description: North Mankato, Minnesota : Capstone Press, 2024. | Series: You choose: great escapes | Includes bibliographical references. | Audience: Ages 8-12. | Audience: Grades 4-6. | Summary: An interactive Civil War adventure where the reader determines their fate during a daring escape from a Confederate prison.
Identifiers: LCCN 2023031052 (print) | LCCN 2023031053 (ebook) | ISBN 9781669061250 (hardcover) | ISBN 9781669061335 (paperback) | ISBN 9781669061298 (pdf) | ISBN 9781669061342 (epub)
Subjects: LCSH: Plot-your-own stories. | CYAC: United States—History—Civil War, 1861-1865—Fiction. | Prisoner-of-war camps—Fiction. | Escapes—Fiction. | Plot-your-own stories. | LCGFT: Choose-your-own stories. | Novels.
Classification: LCC PZ7.G963 Can 2024 (print) | LCC PZ7.G963 (ebook) | DDC [Fic]—dc23
LC record available at https://lccn.loc.gov/2023031052
LC ebook record available at https://lccn.loc.gov/2023031053

Editorial Credits
Editor: Christopher Harbo; Designer: Sarah Bennett; Media Researcher: Svetlana Zhurkin; Production Specialist: Katy LaVigne

Image Credits
Alamy: Digital Image Library, 45, History and Art Collection, 99, Pictures Now, 21, Reading Room 2020, 16; Associated Press: North Wind Picture Archives, cover, 91; Getty Images: Hulton Archive, 74, mikroman6, 38; Library of Congress: 6, 8, 10, 12, 27, 55, 60, 73, 78, 80, 83, 97, Geography and Map Division, 62; Newscom: AiWire/Heritage Images/Heritage Art/Thomas C. Roche, 71; Shutterstock: Beaufortitude, 67, Dustie, 89, Everett Collection, 9, EWY Media, 105, holwichaikawee (jail background), cover, back cover and throughout, Lynne Ann Mitchell, 34, Mark Carrel, 51, Nik Merkulov (grunge background), 6 and throughout, Robert Crow, 49; Superstock: ClassicStock, 102; XNR Productions: 106

Printed and bound in China. 6274

CONTENTS

ABOUT YOUR ADVENTURE

YOU have been captured! The Civil War (1861–1865) has torn the United States in half, and you are locked in a Confederate prison. The good news is that you're alive. The bad news is that life as a prisoner of war is harsh. Not everyone will make it out alive. Escape will be difficult, but you have to try. YOU CHOOSE how to make your escape. Will you succeed or fail? Turn the page to find out.

Chapter One sets the scene. Then you choose which path to read. Follow the directions at the bottom of the page as you read the stories. The decisions you make will change your outcome. After you finish one path, go back and read the others for new perspectives and more adventures.

Turn the page to begin your adventure.

Abraham Lincoln became the president of the United States on March 4, 1861.

CHAPTER 1

CIVIL WAR PRISONS

In 1860, Abraham Lincoln is elected President of the United States, and you hold your breath. You know southern states fear he will abolish slavery, which could lead to war.

Sure enough, South Carolina secedes from the Union in December 1860. Before long, more southern states follow. In all, eleven states—South Carolina, Mississippi, Florida, Alabama, Georgia, Louisiana, Texas, Virginia, Arkansas, North Carolina, and Tennessee—form the Confederate States of America.

Then, on April 12, 1861, Confederate forces fire upon Union-held Fort Sumter in South Carolina. The Civil War begins.

Turn the page.

The war lasts longer than everyone thinks it will. In the First Battle of Bull Run in July 1861, Union forces expect to easily overtake the Confederate capital of Richmond, Virginia. They hope to put a quick end to the war. Instead, the Union is driven back. The Union sees nearly 3,000 dead, and the Confederates lose nearly 2,000. The war is bloodier than anyone imagined and is far from over.

Union and Confederate armies fighting during the First Battle of Bull Run

Former enslaved people escaping to the Union army lines after the Emancipation Proclamation went into effect

Over the next year, more battles ensue. In September 1862, forces collide along Antietam Creek in Maryland. More than 22,000 on both sides are dead, wounded, or captured. But the battle is a Union victory.

The victory at Antietam leads President Lincoln to issue the Emancipation Proclamation in January 1863. Lincoln declares that all enslaved people in rebellious states are free. The Union cause shifts from preserving the Union to ending slavery.

Turn the page.

Camp Douglas in Chicago, Illinois, began holding Confederate prisoners in February 1862.

Since the war's beginning, prison camps have been set up on both sides to hold captured soldiers. An exchange system allows for prisoners of war to be swapped quickly. Prison camps are largely empty in 1862, with most prisoners exchanged within a few days.

But, in 1863, the Confederacy refuses to exchange Black Union soldiers. The Confederates classify Black prisoners of war as runaway enslaved people. The Confederates say the Black soldiers should be returned to their enslavers rather than be exchanged.

President Lincoln suspends the exchange system until the Confederates agree to treat Black prisoners and white prisoners as equal. Prisons fill up. Prisoners suffer under crowded conditions, lack of food, and the spread of sickness. Without exchanges, there's not much hope in sight for the prisoners.

Back when the war started, you never dreamed you'd become a prisoner of war. But now you are one, and escape is always on your mind. You've heard rumors about successful escapes. But you've also witnessed what happens when an escapee is caught. They can face severe punishment—or even worse. But with sickness spreading and starvation setting in, escape might be your only means of survival.

To be a prisoner held at Libby Prison, turn to page 13.
To be an imprisoned Unionist, turn to page 39.
To be a prisoner headed for Andersonville, turn to page 75.

LIBBY PRIS N.

CHAPTER 2

LOCKED IN LIBBY PRISON

It is 1863. You are a Union officer fighting in the Civil War. During the Battle of Chickamauga in Georgia, you are captured by the Confederates. They throw you into a wagon and haul you to Libby Prison.

Libby Prison is an old tobacco warehouse along the James River in Richmond, Virginia. The moment you arrive, you begin dreaming of escape. The prison is old, damp, and crowded. You and more than 2,000 other prisoners are crammed into the upper two floors. The windows have no panes, just bars. In winter, cold wind and snow whip into the building. In summer, heat, humidity, and rain seep in.

Turn the page.

You sleep on a mat on the floor, with barely enough room to roll over. You have no extra clothing, just the uniform you were wearing when captured. But you're lucky. Some prisoners have hardly any clothes at all. They tie rags around their waists.

And there's very little food. You are fed only once a day—just a little bread, and maybe some meat if you're lucky. December sets in, and you hope you survive the winter.

One day, you are approached by two prisoners, Colonel Rose and Major Hamilton. They seem tired and dirtier than most prisoners. But they are also brimming with excitement.

"We know you have been longing to escape," Rose says.

"And we'd like to offer you a great opportunity," Hamilton adds.

You nod, interested. They tell you they have an escape plan. This past month, they've spent nights carefully removing bricks from the kitchen fireplace on the first floor. Then they were able to drop through the fireplace into the cellar below.

"We are planning to dig a tunnel from the cellar out into the old tobacco shed in the yard," Rose tells you.

"But we need all the help we can get," says Hamilton.

"I'm in!" you agree.

Rose and Hamilton swear you to secrecy. They arrange three five-man teams. Every third night, you and your team take out the fireplace bricks, drop down into the cellar, and dig. You have only one small chisel, a couple of jackknives, and your bare hands.

Turn the page.

A cross-section of Libby Prison shows the hidden entrance to the cellar that prisoners used to dig a tunnel.

The cellar is pitch-dark. And the smell is horrible. The stink of sewage makes you gag.

But the worst is the rats. Hundreds of rats! They scurry over your body as you chisel away. Sometimes they even nibble at your hands and feet. The cellar earns the nickname "Rat Hell."

The work is slow going. At this rate, it'll take months to dig the tunnel. And it's too risky to talk to your teammates, so you work in silence.

One night, you hear guards approaching.

"Thought I heard something," says one guard.

You and your teammates lie completely silent as the guards enter the cellar. A rat scampers across your face. Your nose twitches. Once, twice. Uh-oh. You are going to sneeze. You try as hard as you can to hold it in. Then it happens. *Achoo!*

Luckily, just then one of the guards lets out a shout. "Ahhh! A rat bit me!"

"Let's get outta here," says the other.

The guards leave. You're safe for now, but you feel uneasy. If you keep digging and you're caught, you could be executed. Plus, you're not sure you can endure Rat Hell anymore. Maybe there's a better—and quicker—way to escape.

To keep working on the tunnel, turn to page 18.
To find another way to escape, turn to page 21.

You want to finish what you started, so you keep digging the tunnel. After three failed attempts, you and the other diggers are about to give up.

Then one day, Colonel Rose tells you they have made progress on a new tunnel. They are certain this is the one.

You set to work again. Then one night, another digger wakes you with news of an emergency meeting in the kitchen.

When you arrive in the kitchen, Rose tells you and the others the tunnel is complete.

"I broke ground near the tobacco shed!" he says. "And then I just walked out the gate."

"Let's go!" someone says.

"It's too close to morning. Let's wait until tonight," someone else argues.

That night, you and the others creep to the kitchen, drop down into the cellar, and squeeze through the tunnel. The tunnel is narrow, and you have to wriggle your body to get through. And it's long. Just when you feel you might suffocate, you break through to open air. You slip into the tobacco shed where other prisoners are gathered.

Rose pokes his head out the shed door. "Coast is clear!"

You walk quickly out of the shed, through the gate, and into the streets of Richmond. You are free!

But not quite. Richmond is still Confederate territory.

"Let's buddy up," says Danny, one of your teammates.

Turn the page.

You and Danny make your way through Richmond, heading out of the city. Dawn is breaking. Up ahead, you see a couple of men on a street corner. You want to veer away, but they've seen you.

"Act natural," you mutter to Danny as you pass.

"You look like a pair of Yanks!" one of the men yells.

You don't know what to do. If you keep going, you might look suspicious. But if you stop and try to convince them you're Confederates, you might give yourselves away.

To stop and convince them, turn to page 23.
To keep going, turn to page 24.

You think there must be an easier way to escape, so you return to your miserable existence at the prison. You pass the time by playing chess on the floor with other prisoners. Sometimes you act out plays and sing songs. You'd rather be anywhere else, but it's still better than chipping away at the tunnel surrounded by rats.

All the prisoners look forward to mail day when guards hand out packages from family. The packages often contain food and clothing.

Prisoners passing time in one of the overcrowded rooms in Libby Prison

Turn the page.

On one mail day, you receive a package. You are about to tear it open when you realize it has already been opened. And there's no food inside. Looking around, you notice everyone else is disappointed too.

"The guards are stealing our food!" you mutter to another prisoner. You know you need to get out of here soon, or you could starve to death. You need to plan your escape, and fast.

You have a few ideas. You could fake your own death. After the guards carry your body out, you could make a run for it. Or you could attempt to crawl out one of the windows and drop to the ground to freedom. Each option has risks, but they are risks you're willing to take.

To fake your death, turn to page 25.
To crawl out a window, turn to page 27.

You pause and grin at the men. "We ain't no Yanks!" you say.

"Then where are you headed at this hour in such smelly clothes?" one of the men growls.

You realize the jig is up and burst into a run. But you are weak from your prison days. So is Danny. In seconds, the men tackle both of you.

The men shout, "Got some Yanks!"

Then you hear the pounding of feet. You wriggle your head around and look up into the face of a prison guard. He recognizes you.

The guard drags you and Danny back to the dungeon in Libby Prison. All you can hope is that the other escapees had better luck.

THE END

To read another adventure, turn to page 11.
To learn more about escapes during the Civil War, turn to page 103.

You and Danny keep walking, ignoring the men. One of them starts after you. You can hear his footsteps stomping behind you.

"If we keep heading outta town, he might get even more suspicious," Danny whispers.

"Let's try to lose him," you agree.

You take a left. Then another left. Then a right. At last, his footsteps fade, and you continue on a more direct path out of the city.

Out in the country, you stay off the roads and make your way through the wilderness. Soon, you come to a wide river. Crossing it will bring you closer to the Union lines. The water looks calm, but you know there might be currents.

"Maybe we should find a better place to cross?" Danny suggests.

To cross the river, turn to page 29.
To find a better place to cross, turn to page 30.

You share your plan with some of your closest friends at the prison. Then, when the guards bring in food rations, you break into a horrible cough. The next day, you lie on your mattress, moaning and wheezing.

"Does he need to go to the hospital?" one of the guards asks, pointing at you.

"I'm fine," you whisper.

The next morning, when the guards are out of sight, you powder your face with flour to make yourself look deathly pale. Your friends wrap rags around your ankles and wrists under your clothes. That way, the guards won't feel your pulse when they carry you out.

"He's dead!" one of your friends cries to the guards.

You hold absolutely still as the guards peer at you.

Turn the page.

"Get him outta here," another friend says. "Or we might all catch whatever he had!"

The guards lift your body and carry you to the Dead House. It's a shack where bodies are kept before they're buried. You wait for the perfect moment to sneak out.

Then you hear a ruckus outside. The shouting intensifies. A fight has broken out. Maybe now is your chance to break away? Or maybe you should wait until dark.

To make a run for it, turn to page 36.
To wait until dark, turn to page 37.

Union prisoners behind the barred windows of Libby Prison

The windows of Libby Prison are high and have bars. But the frames are made from wood. You eye the windows carefully. Maybe you can break the frame and slide out the window. You are so skinny from lack of food that you could probably slide through easily.

One night, you decide to inspect the window more closely. After the night guard finishes his rounds, you make your move.

You slip toward the window and jiggle the bars to see if the window could loosen. Then you hear footsteps behind you. You freeze.

Turn the page.

"Hey!" a guard yells.

You know you aren't supposed to go anywhere near the windows. Prison rules.

"I was just looking outside!" you explain. "I forgot the rule!"

Then you hear the crack of a gun.

Pain explodes in your shoulder. You fall to the floor, flailing. Guards rush toward you and haul you to your feet, ignoring your injured shoulder. You howl in pain as they march you to the prison dungeon. You won't be making another escape attempt for a long time.

THE END

To read another adventure, turn to page 11.

To learn more about escapes during the Civil War, turn to page 103.

"We need to get out of Confederate territory," you say. "Let's cross the river."

You put one foot into the water. Brrr! The water is cold. You plunge in and hope your body gets used to the icy temperature.

You pump your arms and kick your legs, making good progress. Danny is ahead of you, nearing the opposite shore. If he can make it, you can too.

Then the water pulls at your legs. A strong current grabs you and swirls you downstream. You shout, but your mouth fills with water. Soon, your entire body is swallowed by the river.

THE END

To read another adventure, turn to page 11.
To learn more about escapes during the Civil War, turn to page 103.

You and Danny head west, picking your way through wooded areas. You have no food, so you gather berries, hoping they're not poisonous. But you can't survive on berries alone.

That evening, you set up camp deep in the woods. You and Danny are shivering in the cold air, so you build a fire. You know the smoke is a risk, but it's dark and quiet out here. Hopefully there's no one for miles.

While you are warming by the fire, a twig snaps. You freeze. A Black man emerges through the trees.

"Saw the smoke, so I came to check it out. What are you doing here?" he demands.

You have no choice but to tell him. You hope he'll be sympathetic.

"We're Yankees, heading to Union lines," you say.

"You better steer clear of the house out yonder," he says, pointing into the woods. "The woman who lives there will turn you in for sure."

You thank him, and he continues on his way. The next day, you continue through the woods until you reach a dirt road. At the end of it sits a cozy white house. Smoke swirls from the chimney. And the smell of food wafts to your nose. You are starving.

Danny sways, and you catch him.

"I'm so weak," he says. "Maybe the woman who lives there will give us some food?"

"But the man said to avoid her," you say.

"Couldn't we try to convince her we're Confederates?" Danny pleads.

To keep going, turn to page 32.
To stop at the house, turn to page 33.

You continue past the house and into the woods. Soon, you feel lost and weak with hunger. You and Danny sit down next to a tree to rest.

Suddenly, you hear footsteps crashing through the woods. Soon, Confederate soldiers surround you. A woman with them points at you.

"That's them!" the woman says. "I saw them near my road. I thought they looked suspicious."

"Escaped from Libby Prison, I'll bet," one of the soldiers says.

"They almost made it too," another says. "The Union lines are just a couple miles away."

Your heart sinks. You were so close, but now it's back to Libby Prison for you.

THE END

To read another adventure, turn to page 11.
To learn more about escapes during the Civil War, turn to page 103.

You approach the house.

"Hello?" you call.

A woman appears on the porch, rifle in hand. "Who are you? What do you want?"

"We are soldiers on our way to Richmond," you say.

"Can you spare a bite to eat?" Danny pleads.

The woman's eyes narrow. "Confederate soldiers?"

"Yes," you lie.

She scans you up and down, her nose wrinkling at the sight of your ragged clothes. "It looks like you've seen better days," she says.

"That's for sure," you agree.

"Just a bite to eat and we'll be on our way," Danny says.

Turn the page.

Your heart thumps as she stares at you both. Then she opens the door. "Come on in."

You and Danny sit down at the kitchen table. The woman gives you plates of grits with stale biscuits. She never lets go of her rifle, and you feel prickles down your back. At any moment, she could figure out who you really are. And then you'd be doomed.

"I don't have much," she says, nodding at the plates of food. "This war has been brutal on us."

But to you it's a feast. You and Danny are so busy stuffing your mouths that there's no time to talk. And the less you talk, the better.

When you are done eating, you thank the woman and make your way to the door.

"Wait," she says.

You freeze.

"The Union camps are just over yonder, past the ravine to the north," she says. "You better avoid that area."

You try not to smile too widely as you thank her again. You and Danny pretend to head south, in case the woman is watching. Then, when you are out of sight of the house, you double back and head toward the ravine. Soon, you see the Union camp, tents spread out and soldiers in blue dotting the landscape. You are free at last.

THE END

To read another adventure, turn to page 11.
To learn more about escapes during the Civil War, turn to page 103.

You peer out the door of the Dead House. The guards are wrestling a prisoner to the ground. You wonder if he tried to escape too.

Now is your chance. You slip through the door, scurry out of the prison yard, and head for the edge of the city. When you reach the countryside, you slow your pace and get your bearings. You've heard that the Union army is near Richmond, so you head north, stopping often to rest.

After two days, you spot men in blue uniforms gathered near the road. You give them your name and rank, and they take you to the captain. He arranges transport to take you home. Your escape from Libby Prison is a success!

THE END

To read another adventure, turn to page 11.
To learn more about escapes during the Civil War, turn to page 103.

You decide it's best to wait until dark. The ruckus outside soon ends, and you are left in silence. Just you and the other bodies. You settle against a wall, as far away from the bodies as possible. Then your eyes close, and sleep takes over. When you open your eyes again, it is pitch dark. You are chilled to the bone, but your skin is hot. You have a fever!

You try to stand, but your legs won't hold you. You crawl toward the door but collapse before you reach it. It turns out you will be leaving Libby Prison as a dead body after all.

THE END

To read another adventure, turn to page 11.
To learn more about escapes during the Civil War, turn to page 103.

CHAPTER 3

IMPRISONED IN CASTLE THUNDER

In 1861, you are a southerner living on a small farm in Virginia. Your family does not enslave people. In fact, you are against slavery. When the Civil War breaks out that April, you don't join the war effort. You, like many people, think the war will be over soon.

But a year later, the war is still raging. The Confederacy issues a draft for all men ages 18 to 35. That's you. But you refuse to comply. You won't fight for something you don't believe in.

One day, there is a knock on your door. It's Confederate officials. You aren't surprised. You knew they'd find you someday. And you're ready to pay a fine.

Turn the page.

But instead of demanding a fine, they arrest you and drag you from your doorstep.

"Got another Unionist," one of the men growls as they throw you into their wagon.

"Where are you taking me?" you ask.

"Castle Thunder," one answers.

Castle? That doesn't sound so bad. But wait. Now you remember reading about Castle Thunder in the newspaper. It's no castle at all, but a prison in Richmond.

Castle Thunder is different from other war prisons. It is not just for captured Union soldiers. The prison also holds civilians, deserters, women, and Black soldiers. The women and Black soldiers are held in Whitlock's Warehouse. The rest of you are in the main prison, which is an old warehouse.

Prison life is horrible. The prison is small, and hundreds of you are stuffed together. You never have enough to eat. Fights break out over food. And the guards are mean. One of them is the worst. He yells at and smacks prisoners for no reason.

One day, he yanks on your arm and pulls you to your feet.

"Come with me," he hisses. "Or else!"

You don't want to go anywhere with this guy. You are afraid of the cruelty he might inflict if you are alone with him.

"I wouldn't go with him if I were you," one of the prisoners warns. "The last guy . . . well, we never saw him again."

To go with the guard, turn to page 42.
To stay put, turn to page 44.

You follow the guard down a long hallway and into a small room. You ready yourself for a beating. But he smiles at you, almost pleasantly. He asks you about your farm and about your family. Your heart hammers. You are suddenly afraid for your loved ones.

"I had a talk with a young woman named Josephine," he says. "Do you know her?"

You think hard. You remember a girl from school named Josephine, but you didn't know her very well.

"No, can't say that I do," you say.

"She's a Unionist, just like you," the guard goes on.

You shake your head wildly. "I'm not—"

"Sure you are," he interrupts, glaring at you. "That's why you're here, right?"

You don't know what to say. You don't want to anger him.

"Josephine wants to help you get out of here," he says.

Your mouth drops open as you stare at him.

He lowers his voice. "And so do I."

You shake your head again. He must be tricking you. He must want to catch you in the act, to punish you even more. You've heard about the cellar that the worst prisoners are thrown into. No way.

But what if he's telling the truth? You could miss a chance to escape.

To refuse his help, turn to page 47.
To accept, turn to page 49.

"No, sir," you say. "I'm not going anywhere with you!"

The guard looks shocked. He raises his arm as if to strike you, then he spins on his heel and stomps away.

You can't help but wonder what the guard wanted with you. You start watching him closely, wondering if his meanness is all an act. But you'll never know.

Food rations lessen. Fights break out. Every night you go to bed hungry. And every morning, you wake up with thoughts of escape. The guards are getting more brutal. If prisoners are caught fighting or stealing food, they get punished horribly. One is strung up by his thumbs. Another is beaten with a stick.

You know you need to get out of here. Fast.

Sometimes Richmond women visit the prison on mercy visits. They bring food, blankets, and clothing. You look forward to their visits. It's nice to see people who aren't prisoners or guards.

One day, a young woman visits. She hands out blankets, socks, and food. When she gives you a bowl of custard, she whispers, "From Elizabeth Van Lew. Mansion on Church Hill."

Elizabeth Van Lew

Turn the page.

You are puzzled. You don't know anyone by that name. You scarf down the custard as the woman watches you.

"Eat it all," she says.

"I did," you say.

When the woman keeps staring at you, you inspect the bowl and realize it has a false bottom. You remove the bottom to find Confederate money. You slide the bills into your pocket and hand the bowl back to the young woman.

"Thank you," you say.

The money will help you immensely. You could use it to bribe the guards to let you escape. Or you could find a different way to escape and keep it. Having money will help you on the outside.

To bribe the guards, turn to page 51.
To pretend to be sick, turn to page 53.

"Sorry," you say, "but I'm not interested."

He raises his eyebrows. "Okay, then. It's back to prison for you."

He marches you back to your mat. When the others ask what happened, you just shrug. You stay quiet in case the guards are listening. But you still think he was trying to trick you.

One night, another accused Unionist who sleeps next to you doesn't come back from a latrine visit. He's still gone the next day.

"What happened to Joe?" you ask the others.

"I don't know," one man says. "But I saw him talking to that mean guard."

Your heart falls like a rock into your belly. The guard—and Josephine—must have helped him escape! You missed your chance, but you're not going to let another chance pass you by.

Turn the page.

"If you turn the other way when I walk out of here, the money's yours," you say.

"I'd do anything for my family," he agrees.

That night, the guard comes to get you. He lets you out a back door, and you disappear into the night.

Your home isn't far from Richmond, but you can't go back there. The Confederates will just arrest you again. So you head north, through the wilderness, hoping to make it to Union territory. You grow weak with hunger. If only you had some money to buy food. But you have nothing.

After days of walking, you collapse in the woods. You can't get back up again. No one will find you until you are just a pile of bones.

THE END

To read another adventure, turn to page 11.
To learn more about escapes during the Civil War, turn to page 103.

You try an old trick by pretending to be sick. You lie on your mat and moan.

"I need to go to the hospital," you croak to the guards. But they pay no attention to you.

Another prisoner nearby is sick too. He looks awful. His skin is splotchy and his face is peppered with blisters.

"Smallpox!" declares a doctor making the rounds. He turns to the guards. "Get him to the hospital."

"Wait!" you cry from your bed. "I think I have smallpox too!"

But no one seems to care.

After he's gone, another prisoner exclaims softly, "Worked again!"

You roll over. "What do you mean?" you whisper.

Turn the page.

"Josephine told me that you refused to fight because you're against slavery," she says. "And I admire that."

You don't know who Josephine is. You vaguely remember a girl from school with the same name. Could it be her? But you are too tired to talk anymore. You sleep for what seems like days, only rising to eat the food that Elizabeth leaves outside the hidden door.

After a few days, Elizabeth knocks on the door. "I need the room for more escapees," she says. "I can give you addresses of other safe houses. Or I can tell you the best way out of the city so you can head to the Union lines."

To go to another safe house, turn to page 62.
To leave Richmond, turn to page 64.

"I'm going to tear my bedding into strips," you tell him. "And tie them together to make a rope. Then I'll drop the rope out the window and use it to climb down."

He nods. "Great idea! But what will you tie it to?"

"That's where you come in," you say. "You could hold the rope for me. And pull it back in when I'm gone. That will buy me more time with the guards. If they see the rope left behind, they'll know someone has escaped."

"Good thinking," he says.

"Unless you want to escape too?" you ask.

He shakes his head, almost too quickly. "Nah. I have a bad ankle. I wouldn't make it very far even if I did make it out."

Turn the page.

Castle Thunder Prison in 1863

You know you're more likely to get caught if you tell anyone your ideas. "I don't really have a plan," you tell him.

His mouth droops in disappointment.

"And it's not a good idea to escape anyway," you go on.

He turns away angrily. You wonder why he's so mad. But you know it was a good idea not to tell him any of your ideas.

Days come and go, and you weigh your options. Servants come in to do the washing. You begin following them on the sly, watching their movements. You think you could disguise yourself as a servant pretty easily.

One day, you pull a hat low over your face, grab a bucket, and fall in line. None of the guards notice you. You follow them to the basement. Then you veer away and duck into a corner.

When night falls, you emerge and walk calmly out the prison doors. If anyone sees you, they'll think you're just a servant leaving work. But no one is around. Keeping your hat low, you break into a run. Your disguise worked, and you're free.

THE END

To read another adventure, turn to page 11.
To learn more about escapes during the Civil War, turn to page 103.

You follow Elizabeth's directions to head through the woods and then cross the James River. Along the way, a teenage girl steps in front of your path. You wonder what she is doing out at this time of night.

"I know who you are," she says.

"Who are you?" you ask. You move to the side to go around her, but she steps into your path.

"You were just at the Van Lews'," she says.

Your heart skips. Who is this girl? How does she know you were at the Van Lews'? She looks tough and strong, but maybe you can outrun her.

"Come with me," she says. "I have a safe house. And an offer for you."

You think you should run, but you're intrigued.

To follow her, go to page 65.

To run, turn to page 67.

You follow the girl, your eyes twitching about just in case someone is following. But you don't see anyone. She tells you her name is Amara.

"I know Josephine," she says pointedly.

Elizabeth Van Lew mentioned the name Josephine too.

"Who is Josephine?" you ask.

"She's been watching you. She's a spy. Just like me. And just like you."

"I'm not a spy," you protest.

"Shh." Amara looks around quickly, and then leads you into a small house. Several children are gathered in front of the fireplace. "These are my siblings," she says.

"You live here alone with them?" you ask.

Turn the page.

She nods. "No one would ever suspect me," she says, whispering so the kids don't hear. You go into the small kitchen, and she points down at the floorboards. "There's a small room under the floor. You can stay there."

When you don't say anything, she looks at you. "Are you going to join us, or what?"

You hesitate. She wants you to work with her as a spy. If you accept, maybe you could help the Union and bring an end to this awful war. Then again, you were really hoping to get out of the South and make a new life for yourself.

To accept, turn to page 69.
To leave the South, turn to page 71.

You shake your head quickly and run. The girl shouts after you, but you keep running. You only slow when you reach the woods.

Then you see train tracks, and you decide to follow them. Following the tracks will ensure you don't get lost.

Turn the page.

After traveling for a while, you see a train. A few workers stand near it, so you swerve into the nearby trees. You hope the workers won't see you.

The train is pointing north, the direction you are going. When you see your chance, you run and leap into a dark car. You hope you are alone.

You're in luck. It's just you and some sacks of flour. Perfect. You hide between the flour sacks and wait. Then the train starts moving. The rhythm lulls you to sleep.

When the train stops several hours later, you wake and poke your head out. No one. You leap off the train, unseen. You can't believe your luck. You just got a free ride north! You make your way to the Union lines and to safety.

THE END

To read another adventure, turn to page 11.
To learn more about escapes during the Civil War, turn to page 103.

"I want to do what I can to end this war," you tell Amara. "And end slavery."

Amara claps her hands. "We need brave people like you," she says. "I'll take you back to Elizabeth's in the morning."

Elizabeth Van Lew is surprised but glad to see you. "I have an urgent mission for you," she says. "Are you up for it?"

You nod eagerly.

"I've discovered that many of the prisoners in Richmond are being sent to other prisons deeper south. I think the Union should know. Will you take this message to General Benjamin Butler?"

She hands you a sheet of paper. But you see nothing written on it. When you look at her, puzzled, she laughs.

Turn the page.

"It's written in citrus ink," she says. "When you shine light on it, you can read it."

Wow. You are amazed at her cleverness. You just hope you are the right person for the job. You make your way across the James River and head north. You successfully deliver the message to General Butler. Van Lew is impressed by your stealth and quickness. You become one of the main couriers of the spy ring, carrying messages to the Union.

One day, your luck runs out. You are caught and sentenced to death for treason against the Confederacy. But you know you did good work and that you served your country until the end.

THE END

To read another adventure, turn to page 11.
To learn more about escapes during the Civil War, turn to page 103.

If you work as a spy for the Union, you risk being caught. You don't want to go back to Castle Thunder and be strung up by your thumbs. Or worse, be executed.

"I can't risk it," you tell Amara.

Her shoulders fall in disappointment. She turns away from you. "The best way out of the city is to cross the James River. Go through the woods. Find a man named Jonas. He'll row you across."

Richmond and the James River during the Civil War

Turn the page.

You thank her and head through the woods toward the James River. Onshore, you see a Black man with a rowboat. When you hand him a coin and tell him you know Amara, he nods.

"After we cross the river, head west for a mile," he says. "Then you'll see a path that heads north. Follow that to a house with a yellow shed."

You get into the rowboat, eyes scanning the shore. You know you could be caught at any moment.

But you make it across safely. When you get to the house with the yellow shed, the woman who lives there offers to drive you closer to the Union lines. You hide in the back of her wagon underneath some hay. As you travel, you think about the bravery of all the people who helped you. You don't feel very brave at all.

Union soldiers in a camp near Brandy Station, Virginia

When you make it to the North, you immediately join the Union army. You want to help the Union the way the southern spies helped you.

THE END

To read another adventure, turn to page 11.

To learn more about escapes during the Civil War, turn to page 103.

Confederate soldiers guarding Union prisoners
of war on Belle Isle in Richmond, Virginia

CHAPTER 4

ANDERSONVILLE HORROR

It's 1864, and you are a prisoner at Belle Isle in Virginia. The prison is miserable, with thousands of prisoners crowded onto a small island with almost no shelter from the weather.

In March, you feel a ray of hope when Union forces launch the Battle of Walkerton in King and Queen County, Virginia. The Union plans to break through Confederate defenses and liberate Belle Isle. But the offensive fails, and you remain a prisoner.

Then you hear that you might be transferred to a new prison. The newly built prison is called Camp Sumter, near Andersonville, Georgia. Most just call it "Andersonville."

Turn the page.

You wait anxiously to be transferred. The new prison must be much better than Belle Isle.

At last, you and a few hundred others are loaded onto train cars that take you south to Georgia. That night, the train slows to a stop.

"All out!" calls one of the guards.

As you get off, the guards tell you to sleep by the tracks and that you'll be loaded back onto the train in the morning. You think it is a weird order, but sleeping under the stars sounds great—at least until the mosquitoes arrive!

Since you can't sleep, you start thinking. Maybe you could slither away from the tracks and escape. There are a lot of guards but even more prisoners. And the night is dark, the moon just a sliver. Maybe now is the time.

To attempt an escape, go to page 77.
To stay with the transport, turn to page 78.

Escape seems like it might be easy. But you have to be patient. You wriggle inch by inch toward the edge of the sleeping bodies. The guard assigned to your section walks back and forth along the tracks. But his pace keeps slowing, and you know he's getting tired. Then, at dawn, he sits down next to the train, gun across his lap. His head drops forward. This is your chance.

You scurry to your feet and run as quietly as you can, heading for the swath of trees near the tracks. But your steps sound as loud as thunder in the quiet night.

"Stop!" the guard yells.

You are almost to the trees. Then you hear the click of his gun. He's going to shoot. Maybe you can dodge the shot by jumping headlong into the trees. Or maybe you should just surrender.

To jump into the trees, turn to page 81.
To surrender, turn to page 82.

If you try to escape, you risk getting caught and killed. So you stay with the transport. Your only hope is that Andersonville isn't so bad. And maybe you'll get exchanged. Or maybe the war will finally end.

But your hopes are dashed the minute you arrive at Andersonville. The prison is a mud pit filled with falling-down tents. There's no shelter from the heat or rain. A slimy stream runs through the prison camp. It's too polluted to drink from. Most prisoners use it as a bathroom.

A bird's-eye view of Andersonville

After only a few days, you realize how many around you are dying. They die from starvation or diseases like dysentery and scurvy. Anyone who is still alive is just a skeleton. No one has the energy to escape. Plus, if those who try are caught, they face the wrath of the cruel prison commander, Henry Wirz.

And, almost worse, a group of prisoners called the Andersonville Raiders terrorize other prisoners. They take clothes off prisoners while they are sleeping. They start fights that sometimes turn deadly. And they steal blankets and food.

The prison camp is surrounded by a wall. An inside perimeter called the Dead Line, about 14 feet from the wall, is marked by boards and slats. Any prisoner who crosses the Dead Line will be shot on the spot. But only if the sentries see them.

Turn the page.

Prisoners' tents near the Dead Line in Andersonville

You know you need to escape before you die here. Crossing the Dead Line and scaling the wall would be the quickest way out. Or you could dig a tunnel. But you might die before then.

To cross the Dead Line, turn to page 85.
To dig a tunnel, turn to page 86.

You dive into the trees. A bullet whizzes overhead and clunks against a tree. You scramble to your feet, crashing through the brush. You might be able to lose the guard in the woods.

But then you hear sounds in front of you. And to the right. And to the left. Not just one guard is after you. Now there are many. And you're surrounded.

You stop as they close in on you, rifles raised. You know you'll never see the light of day again, but at least you don't have to endure another day in prison.

THE END

To read another adventure, turn to page 11.
To learn more about escapes during the Civil War, turn to page 103.

You stop running and throw your hands up. "I surrender!" you cry.

The guards grab you and haul you back to the transport train. By now, all the prisoners are awake, watching the guards drag you into the train car. You feel embarrassed for being caught but also somewhat proud of yourself for trying.

"Trying to escape, huh?" a prisoner named Lionel asks as the train starts moving south.

You shrug.

"I know a better way," he whispers. "Bunk next to me tonight."

The train huffs along the tracks. Time moves slowly. You nod off to sleep in the afternoon, getting some rest for tonight.

When everyone is asleep along the tracks again that night, Lionel whispers his plan. You nod eagerly.

Prisoners on a train in Georgia during the Civil War

His idea is to hide under the train. You inch your way under it. In the morning, as other prisoners board the train, you stay hidden.

Then the train begins moving. You lie perfectly still as the train whooshes over you. Adrenaline pumps through your body. If you move even just a bit, the train might catch you and drag you with it.

At last, the train is gone. Above you is just the sky. No one except Lionel is around. You are free!

Turn the page.

But you still need to move north to the Union lines. You know you are deep in the South and have a long way to go.

You and Lionel hike north, avoiding main roads and sleeping in wooded areas. As you move north, the nights get colder. You build fires to stay warm and hope no one sees the smoke.

One night, Lionel cries out in pain. You wake to find him kicking a fiery log that has rolled onto his leg.

You rush to help him put out his smoldering pants. You can see he's badly burned.

Just then, you hear branches breaking. Someone is coming. You should run, but you know Lionel won't be able to walk, let alone run.

"Go!" he hisses. "Save yourself!"

To run, turn to page 87.
To stay with Lionel, turn to page 89.

"You helped me escape, and I won't leave you now," you tell Lionel. He starts to protest again, but you hold your fingers to your lips.

A group of men bursts into the clearing. You nearly collapse in relief at their blue uniforms. Union soldiers!

"Who are you?" one demands. "Confederates? Deserters?"

Regular Union army troops wore dark blue uniforms made of wool.

Turn the page.

You shake your head. "Union prisoners of war," you say. "We escaped from the train transport to Andersonville."

Another soldier whistles. "Good for you. Andersonville is a death trap."

"We've got a wagon over yonder," another soldier says. "Come with us."

The soldiers help Lionel to his feet, and you let him lean on you as you follow the soldiers to their wagon.

At their camp, you rest for a few days and then go home. When you've had enough time to recover, you rejoin your old regiment. You keep fighting for freedom for all.

THE END

To read another adventure, turn to page 11.
To learn more about escapes during the Civil War, turn to page 103.

You've always been a fast runner. It will only take a few seconds to cross the Dead Line. You'd be foolish not to risk it. And you know you'd better do it soon before you grow weaker or get sick.

You keep track of the sentries' movements. They are busiest, and most distracted, at meal time. When the meal carts arrive, you make your move. You leap over the wooden boards marking the border. You're in the Dead Line. You have to run faster than you've ever run before.

But it feels like you're in a dream. Your legs won't move as fast as you want them to.

"Hey!" a guard shouts. You see him reach for his gun, and you know it's all over.

THE END

To read another adventure, turn to page 11.

To learn more about escapes during the Civil War, turn to page 103.

You scout the best place to dig a tunnel. Then you discover you aren't the only one with that idea. You join other diggers, taking turns keeping watch and digging. By now, the prisoner numbers have swelled to nearly 30,000. If your plan succeeds, you're sure no one will miss you.

But the work is slow, and the soft, moist dirt collapses easily. You often have to start over. And all around you, prisoners are dying by the dozens. The bodies are piled onto wagons and carried outside the prison walls. Unless you finish the tunnel quickly, you might be next.

The thought of death gives you an idea. What if you pretended to be dead? You could be carted out with other dead bodies. And it would be easier than digging a tunnel that may never be finished.

To fake your death, turn to page 91.
To keep digging the tunnel, turn to page 93.

There's no use in both of you getting caught. So you wish Lionel well and run as fast as you can through the maze of trees.

But now travel is harder. You have to find food on your own, and it's scarce. You are weak from hunger. And you don't know where you are.

One day, you come across a cabin in the woods. A woman is outside hanging laundry. You don't see anyone else around, so you think it will be safe to ask for food and directions.

As you walk up a path leading to the cabin, the woman turns toward you. "You sure are a sorry sight," she says. "Are you looking for food?"

You nod your head. "I'd be obliged," you say.

Inside the cabin, the woman serves you the best meal you've had in months. You know you'll be able to travel farther on a full stomach.

Turn the page.

Just as you are about to take your leave, the door crashes open. Four men burst in, pointing rifles at you.

"This is him," the woman says. "Union, I bet."

You look at her questioningly.

"I saw you coming," she says. "And figured you were a Union escapee. So I sent my son for help."

"Thanks for the meal," you mutter. The men grab your arms and dump you into their wagon. They take you to the Confederates, who send you to Andersonville prison.

Andersonville is a swampy prison so infested with diseases that you die within days.

THE END

To read another adventure, turn to page 11.
To learn more about escapes during the Civil War, turn to page 103.

Union prisoners of war endured miserable conditions at Andersonville.

Faking your death is easy. You are so thin and malnourished that you look sick anyway. You spend a day moaning in your tent so others around you are convinced too. Then you fall silent.

"Do you think he might've died?" one of your neighbors asks. "I don't hear moaning anymore."

"Maybe he's just asleep," another says. You hold your breath as they bend over you.

"Better get the guards to get the body outta here," your neighbor says.

Turn the page.

You continue your death stance as the guards load you onto a wagon with other bodies. It's all you can do not to gag. Then you are carried out of camp and tossed into a shallow hole. Soon, all is silent.

Now is your chance to crawl out and make a run for it. But then you hear voices approaching.

"Better make sure they're all dead," one says. "I heard some prisoners have been trying to escape this way."

Uh-oh. As you open your eyes a crack to see what the guards are doing, one approaches you with his bayonet. In that instant, you know your fate is sealed.

THE END

To read another adventure, turn to page 11.

To learn more about escapes during the Civil War, turn to page 103.

You continue digging the tunnel, night after night. Finally, it is completed. You wriggle through and emerge on the other side of the prison wall. Freedom!

But you didn't realize how barren the landscape would be. No trees for miles. No shelter. Surely the guards can see you out here.

"Scatter and run!" you call to the other tunnelers. If you scatter, maybe they'll only catch one or two of you. And you hope it's not you.

As you take off toward the horizon, you hear footsteps behind you. When you glance back, a big brown dog leaps on your back. You tumble to the ground. Then a guard pulls you to your feet.

"Good dog," he says, patting the dog's head. He turns to you. "Back to prison!"

You hope the other diggers have made it. But you soon learn the rest, like you, were caught.

Turn the page.

You won't try tunnelling again. But the taste of freedom makes you want it more than ever.

One night, you wake to someone pulling your blanket from your body. When you sit up, you find yourself surrounded by a few men. Raiders.

You stand, ready to fight them off. Then a Raider leader named Delaney steps forward.

"I recognize you," he says. "You tried to escape. I admire that."

"Just give me back my blanket," you growl.

He ignores you. "Join us," he says. "We've got food and warm clothing. We might even help you escape."

You hesitate. You don't like that they steal from others. But you're tired, cold, and hungry. If you join the Raiders, you'll be warm and well-fed.

To join the Raiders, go to page 95.
To fight back, turn to page 98.

Survival is your main goal at this point. And by joining up with the Raiders, you're bound to survive.

"When do I start?" you ask, smiling.

Delaney laughs and hands over your blanket. "Come on. Camp by us."

The Raiders have a huge tent that can fit almost a hundred prisoners.

"The tent was made with stolen materials," Delaney tells you proudly.

You settle into your new place with the Raiders. You don't enjoy stealing. Not at all. So you agree to be a lookout. You keep an eye out for guards while the others do the raiding.

And you can't say you mind the loot they bring back. The blankets, shoes, clothing, and food certainly make life easier in Andersonville.

Turn the page.

One day, Delaney comes to you. "We have a problem," he says. He tells you that another group has formed. They're called the Regulators.

"The Confederates gave them the authority to arrest us," he says. "So we have to be even quicker. And on the lookout every minute."

But that night, before you can even attempt a raid, the Regulators surround your headquarters. You try to fight them off, but there are too many of them. The next morning, you are put on trial. Your fellow prisoners are the jury. The angriest are the ones you stole from. You feel terrible for your actions. You vow never to steal again.

You tell your story to the jury, hoping they'll let you go. Lucky for you, they give you a mild punishment—the stocks. You are forced to sit with your hands and feet bound, while the other prisoners mock you and throw things at you.

Six leaders of the Raiders were punished by hanging as a lesson to the entire camp.

But it could be worse. Delaney and five other leaders are sentenced to death.

You don't make another escape attempt. You don't want to push your luck any further. Plus, the horrors of Andersonville are a punishment you deserve.

THE END

To read another adventure, turn to page 11.
To learn more about escapes during the Civil War, turn to page 103.

"I will never join you!" you cry. You lunge at the Raider who has your blanket. He flies through the air when you push him, landing on the ground with a thud.

"Someone's coming! Let's get outta here!" Delaney orders.

You snatch your blanket and crawl back under your tent. But you can't sleep. At dawn, you grab a pen and write down what happened in your journal. Then you take it to a guard.

You don't expect much to come of it. But days later, you hear that the prison's commander, Henry Wirz, has cut off rations until the Raiders are caught. And, because of your excellent writing skills, he offers you a job keeping prison records. You don't want to work with the Confederates, but if you do, you might find a way to escape.

To take the job, go to page 99.
To refuse, turn to page 101.

Henry Wirz

Before you begin working for Wirz, you must take an oath of allegiance. You do so, even though you might be shunned by other prisoners. Then you start working as a clerk. You keep records of the prisoners' ages, places of origin, and ranks. You are glad for something to do. You often get your food rations first too.

Some of the Confederate soldiers you work with aren't so bad. You even make friends with some of them. One, named John, tells you he hates the war. At this point, you do too. You just want to be home and away from this prison.

Turn the page.

So one day, you tell John about your longing to escape. You laugh a little, hoping he doesn't report you. Instead, he offers to help you.

You are hesitant to trust him. But you think of him as your friend, so you accept his help.

One night, you hide in a small cart filled with hospital rags and supplies. John wheels the cart out of the prison and toward the laundry. Then the cart stops. You hear muffled voices. Your heart thunders. But then the cart moves again. Soon, John lifts the rags from your face.

"Go!" he whispers. "Be free."

You escape into the night. When this war is finally over, you vow to look John up and give him a proper thanks.

THE END

To read another adventure, turn to page 11.
To learn more about escapes during the Civil War, turn to page 103.

You don't want anything to do with Wirz, or the rest of the Confederates. You politely refuse the offer. Instead, you join a group called the Regulators. They find and arrest Raiders. One night, you and the other Regulators surround the Raiders' camp, drag them out, and tie them up. Then they are put on trial, with a jury of other prisoners.

At last, you and the others can sleep soundly without the Raiders prowling around. And you do sleep, long and hard. When you wake up, you are burning with fever. Days pass. When you don't get better, you are carried to the hospital. You'll spend your last days there. You didn't escape, but at least you didn't work for the Confederates. You can die with a clear conscience.

THE END

To read another adventure, turn to page 11.

To learn more about escapes during the Civil War, turn to page 103.

General Lee and General Grant meet to sign the terms of the Confederate surrender.

CHAPTER 5

TRUE CIVIL WAR ESCAPES

In April 1865, Confederate General Robert E. Lee surrendered to Union General Ulysses S. Grant. The Civil War effectively came to an end. War prisons began releasing their prisoners. But the death rates in the prisons had been high. About 56,000 soldiers on both sides died in prisons throughout the war.

Many exciting tales of escape abounded after the war. Some were true, some were not. The stories told in this book are based on real ways that Civil War prisoners tried to escape. Some faked sickness or death. Others dug tunnels to freedom. And some prisoners got help from others.

The Libby Prison breakout is true and documented. It was the greatest escape of the Civil War. The tunnel allowed 109 soldiers to escape. Of those escapees, 59 reached Union lines, 48 were recaptured, and two drowned. Because many considered Libby Prison to be totally "escape-proof," the great escape came as a big surprise to the Confederate guards.

Many soldiers also owed their escapes to helpers on the outside. Elizabeth Van Lew helped Union prisoners escape by hiding them in her secret rooms. She also helped escaped enslaved people and became a spy for the Union. Black Americans—both enslaved and free—also often helped Union prisoners find their way north.

Escape from Andersonville was not easy. Although some managed it, many were too sick and weak to make it very far. Only 351 prisoners were documented to have escaped.

The entrance to the National Prisoner of War Museum in Andersonville, Georgia

Many prisoners still suffered even after they returned home. Some had lingering illness and disease. Others were plagued with nightmares and stress.

In 1998, the National Prisoner of War Museum opened on the site of Andersonville prison camp. The museum tells the many stories of Americans who were prisoners of war—and those who escaped.

CIVIL WAR PRISON CAMPS MAP

KEY EVENTS OF THE CIVIL WAR

NOVEMBER 6, 1860 Abraham Lincoln is elected president.

DECEMBER 20, 1860 South Carolina secedes from the United States. Ten more states soon follow.

APRIL 12, 1861 The Civil War begins when Confederates fire on U.S. troops at Fort Sumter in South Carolina.

MAY 1861 Richmond, Virginia, becomes the capital of the Confederacy.

JANUARY 1, 1863 President Lincoln issues the Emancipation Proclamation, declaring that all enslaved people in the Confederate states are free.

FEBRUARY 1864 Camp Sumter, or Andersonville, opens as a prisoner-of-war camp.

FEBRUARY 9, 1864 After weeks of digging, 109 Union officers escape Libby Prison through a tunnel.

APRIL 9, 1865 Confederate General Robert E. Lee surrenders to Union General Ulysses S. Grant, bringing about the end of the war.

APRIL 14, 1865 President Lincoln is shot by John Wilkes Booth and dies the next day.

OTHER PATHS TO EXPLORE

- In Chapter 3, your escape is aided by others such as Elizabeth Van Lew, a southerner who helped the Union. Put yourself in the shoes of someone like Van Lew. How would you help escapees stay hidden? How would you keep your friends and neighbors from discovering your secret?

- Many escape stories tell of guards who helped escapees, either because of bribes or friendship. Imagine that you are a guard at Andersonville. How might you help a prisoner escape? How would you get them out of the camp without being caught?

- Civilians often visited Civil War prisons to bring goods to the prisoners. What if you were a civilian visiting the prisoners? What items might you bring to help the prisoners survive or escape?

GLOSSARY

allegiance (uh-LEE-junss)—loyal support for someone or something

draft (DRAFT)—a system of choosing people for required military service

dysentery (DI-sen-tayr-ee)—a serious infection of the intestines that can be deadly; dysentery is often caused by drinking contaminated water

emancipation (i-MAN-si-pay-shuhn)—freedom from enslavement or control

latrine (lah-TREEN)—a toilet or outhouse

malnourished (mal-NUR-ishd)—inadequately fed

regiment (REJ-uh-muhnt)—a large group of soldiers who fight together as a unit

scurvy (SCURV-ee)—a deadly disease caused by lack of vitamin C; scurvy produces swollen limbs, bleeding gums, and weakness

secede (si-SEED)—to formally withdraw from a group or an organization

smallpox (SMAWL-poks)—a disease that spreads easily from person to person, causing chills, fever, and blisters

Unionist (YOON-yuhn-ist)—a southerner who was loyal to the United States rather than to the Confederacy during the Civil War

BIBLIOGRAPHY

Denney, Robert E. *Civil War Prisons & Escapes: A Day-by-Day Chronicle*. New York: Sterling Pub. Co., 1993.

National Park Service. *Andersonville National Historic Site, Georgia*. February 6, 2023. nps.gov/ande/index.htm.

Ryan, David D., ed. *A Yankee Spy in Richmond: The Civil War Diary of "Crazy Bet" Van Lew*. Mechanicsburg, PA: Stackpole Books, 1996.

Varon, Elizabeth R. *Southern Lady, Yankee Spy: The True Story of Elizabeth Van Lew, A Union Agent in the Heart of the Confederacy*. New York: Oxford University Press, 2003.

Wheelan, Joseph. *Libby Prison Breakout: The Daring Escape from the Notorious Civil War Prison*. New York: PublicAffairs, 2010.

READ MORE

Brown, W. N. *Civil War Breakout*. New York: Harper, 2020.

Gale, Ryan. *Fact and Fiction of the Civil War*. Minneapolis: Core Library, 2022.

Parker, Philip. *The Civil War Visual Encyclopedia*. New York: DK Publishing, 2021.

INTERNET SITES

Britannica Kids: American Civil War
kids.britannica.com/kids/article/American-Civil-War/352967

Britannica Kids: Andersonville National Historic Site
kids.britannica.com/kids/article/Andersonville-National-Historic-Site/633153

DK FindOut!: American Civil War
dkfindout.com/us/history/american-civil-war

ABOUT THE AUTHOR

photo by Anda Marie Photography

Jessica Gunderson grew up in the small town of Washburn, North Dakota. She has a bachelor's degree from the University of North Dakota and an MFA in Creative Writing from Minnesota State University, Mankato. She has written more than one hundred books for young readers. Her book *President Lincoln's Killer and the America He Left Behind* won a 2018 Eureka! Nonfiction Children's Book Silver Award. She currently lives in Madison, Wisconsin.

BOOKS IN THIS SERIES

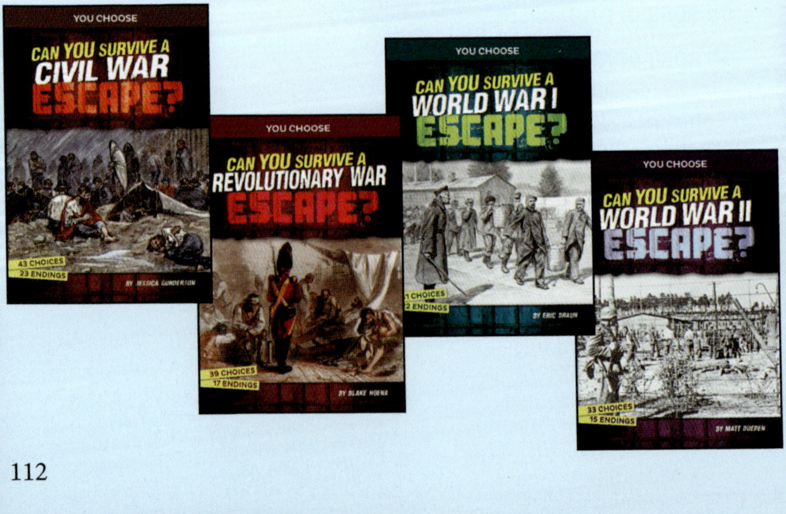